DARK NIGHT OF THE SOUL

How to Stop Feeling Like Sh*t & Develop Mental Toughness in Life

DARK NIGHT OF THE SOUL

WORKBOOK & JOURNAL

Valerie Love
A Butterfly Rising Publication

DARK NIGHT OF THE SOUL - HOW TO STOP FEELING LIKE SH*T & DEVELOP MENTAL TOUGHNESS IN LIFE WORKBOOK & JOURNAL

A Butterfly Rising Publication

Published April 2021

For information visit **www.ValerieLove.com**

ISBN: 9781693391651

Dedication

For you.
You are loved.
You are adored.
You are watched over and looked after.
You are tended to with the utmost of care.
Remember this.
It will save your life.

Disclaimer

Nothing in this book is intended to be mental health or health advice, nor is it intended to treat, diagnose or heal any mental health issue or any physical issue in the body.
Seek support from a mental health care professional you trust if required. Seek care from a health care professional you trust if required.
Take extra good care of yourself.
There's only one of you.
You're precious.

Also by Valerie Love

NO EXCUSES MANIFESTO

10 Steps to Ascend Any Crisis or Dark Night of the Soul and Attain Mental Toughness

SOULGASM

Daily Meditations to Co-Create & Manifest a Bliss-filled Life!

(366 messages & devotions for daily inspiration & insight)

HOW TO TRUST

A Psalms Prayer Journal

40 MONEY MANTRAS

40 Days to Wealth Consciousness!

GOD IS IN LOVE WITH YOU

Allow God's Love to Manifest In Your Life Today!

DIVALICIOUS!

22 Ways to Fall in Love With YourSelf

All books are available at www.ValerieLove.com

Soul Denial

In the year 1990, I fell into a deep, dark hole of a mammoth depression I couldn't shake no matter what methods or techniques I employed. Hopeless, I lie in bed with the curtains drawn, day after wretched day, barely able to function.

I had just given birth to my second child, a gorgeous baby girl. The doctors said I was suffering from postpartum depression. Irrational fears plagued my mind, including the recurring thought and nightmare that someone would bust into my home, grab the baby, put her in the microwave and turn it on.

I couldn't handle my thoughts. At times, my mind was a wild stallion, with no taming in sight. At other times, I was dead inside.

It came to a head one day when I stood before the medicine cabinet and reached for the bottle of 800 milligram Motrin the doctors had given me to help with pain while healing from childbirth.

How many pills would it take to go to sleep and not wake up?

Suddenly, a searing question jolted me out of my mental stupefaction: *who would take care of my babies if I wasn't here?*

The thought of not being there for my nursing baby and toddler son terrified me enough to cause me to yank my hand from the pills and decide to live. That was the beginning of the end of my long dark night of the soul. Unbeknownst to me, I would enter another dark night decades later. For now, let's focus on what brought on the first one: ignoring and denying the soul.

If you're in a dark night of the soul, you may or may not be experiencing it for the same reasons I was. For me, ignoring and denying my soul had been the precursor to pain. There's no way to ignore the soul and thrive spiritually, mentally, emotionally or physically.

Let's go a little deeper.

I was raised in the cult of Jehovah's Witnesses, where I spent 26 years (from age 4 to age 30) of my life doing the best I could to meet the fanatical demands of a man-made religion. For decades I had done what others wanted me to do, without proffering deep attention and honor to what I was called to be and do. At one point, I was a Regular Pioneer (a Jehovah's Witness who commits to knocking on doors and walking the streets for at least 3 hours per day proselytizing for more converts).

From the time I was a tiny tot, before attending school, I was told what to do, and what not to do, all governed by the religion of my upbringing.

The first set of rules weren't avoidable, being a child of a devout recently turned Jehovah's Witness.

No holidays.

We complied.

No birthdays.

We complied.

No short skirts. No immodest clothing.

We complied.

No friends outside the Witness world.

We complied.

When I turned teenage, it was time to make my commitment to serve Jehovah for the rest of my life and symbolize the vow by being baptized at the next Witness convention.

I did that. I was 15.

Shortly thereafter, when I reached high school, they told me not to even think about going to college. It was considered a breeding ground for rampant drug use and gratuitous sex.

I did as I was told and passed on college.

They told me to take up a simple trade in high school that would enable me to get a job when I graduated, being careful to avoid careers that would require too much of me with the forbidden aim of 'worldly' success. Success in this 'world' required time and energy; time and energy that would be better served following the stringent rules of the religion. To avoid the trappings of society, I was told to get a job that would allow me to contribute to the monthly expenses of our family. Later on, when it would be the prescribed time for me to get married, I would either stay home and take care of our children, or work a part time job that contributed to the household. Nothing more.

I did that.

They told me I could only date fellow Jehovah's Witnesses.

I did that.

They told me I could only marry a fellow Jehovah's Witness.

I did that.

They told us, as the newest married couple in the cult, to acquire our own modest apartment and go to all the Jehovah's Witness meetings and out in 'field service' religiously, no matter what.

We did that too.

When we had children, we instructed them as we had been instructed, dutifully dressing them and myself so that the whole family would be at all 5 meetings per week. My husband was right there doing the same.

Over time, a barrage of questions began to flood my mind...

Who's life is this?

Is this the life I want?

Or am I damned to an existence full of what other people demand I do or not do?

Coming to an honest assessment and realization of my situation plunged me into the worst depression.

I did not have the life I wanted.

Nowhere near.

I did not want to do what I was doing, and could find no way out.

Everything in my world was tied to the Witness cult, with no clear path to disentangle myself and no seeming end in sight of the drudgery that had become my daily existence.

I was trapped like a caged rat.

There's more.

Because I was morbidly unhappy, with no high points to look forward to, and no known bliss frequency to tap into, I had to get my kicks in acceptable ways. I chose distractions, rescues and ultimately: burnout.

Distractions showed up as busying myself with all manner of behaviors and habits that would never lead to greatness.

Rescues showed up as repeated attempts to save anyone and everyone, as long as I didn't have to focus on me, my destiny and the incessant call of my soul. If someone was in trouble, I was there, happy to dive right in with limited resources, overextending myself while supplying my blood stream with yet another hit of the adrenaline I was addicted to.

I would live for the opportunity to hurl myself into the next emergency, craving it even. At least it was something to do. I was game for almost anything to break the drone of my monotonous, wearisome, never-ending round of doing the next obligatory thing.

I was on a treadmill that I could find no way to leap from.

Burnout was a habit. My first husband would warn me whenever he saw me 'burning the candle at both ends.' One of his nicknames for me was Florence Nightingale.

I was willing to sacrifice myself. Distractions, rescues and burnout were unconscious, self-contrived diversions from a life I had grown to abhor.

Can you see why, my dear reader, I plunged into the dark night and great depression?

It was inevitable. At some point, I would have to wake up and smell the proverbial coffee. I would have to make hard choices about my life and what I truly desired, from deep within the heart and soul. I was terrified of that reality.

I had never done it before, especially after 26 years of being told what to do from sunup to sundown and every hour in between.

The dark night of the soul had enveloped me.

I slept more. It became harder and harder to wake up in the mornings. I couldn't speak to anyone around me about the truth of what I was going through. They were all Witnesses who would have found my experience alarming and would have promptly reported me to the elders.

I felt utterly alone. Hopeless. Afraid. For a long while.

Until that fateful day when my soul issued an ultimatum: LIVE or DIE.

It didn't care which I chose. There was no judgment in it. The clear command from inside myself was simply to CHOOSE.

Up until the ultimatum, I hadn't chosen to LIVE. REALLY LIVE.

I was existing... prodding myself through one excruciating day to the next.

I wasn't bringing the best of me to anyone, not my kids, my husband or myself.

My soul had taken a back seat to religious propaganda for decades. I'd managed to ignore, avoid or suppress all the inner alarms. I didn't want to face my reality and deal.

Something had to change, otherwise I'd be dead soon enough, and most likely by my own hand.

The Voice saved me. It spoke to me as I lay in bed one day, in a tone louder than I could ignore:

GET UP.
GO OUTSIDE.

The guidance was asking a monumental undertaking of me, considering I was glued to the bed. Even still, I carried out the command. I rose, got in the shower and went outside. The sun fell on my face. The Voice spoke again:

LOOK UP.

I looked up at the powder blue sky, with not a cloud in sight. It was beautiful. Had I not looked up before? I couldn't remember.

WALK.

Was the next command. I did.

BREATHE.

I did that too.

Now, instead of taking orders from the outside and compliantly following, I was receiving guidance from inside myself and happy to follow it.

I was beginning the path to freedom. I left the cult and decided to permanently follow the inner Voice that seemed to have all the right answers for me.

I've never looked back.

Now, as I write these words in 2021, over 30 glorious years later, I can tell you that the dark nights of the soul I've experienced have been surmountable, though they seemed anything but when I was submerged in them.

That first dark night of the soul lasted 7 years. The second dark night of the soul lasted 3. Altogether, I've spent a decade of my life in the dark.

It was hard, but not unwinnable.

This book tells you EXACTLY what I did to ascend the dark nights of the soul, and how you can use what's here as a ladder to your own ascension, if it resonates with you.

Let's now address what a Dark Night of the Soul is.

What Is a Dark Night of the Soul?

For me, it's a period of spiritual darkness that affects mind, body and especially emotions. The dark nights of the soul have been the lowest of the low points in my life.

Even so, they have a purpose.

I shared with you what led up to my first dark night of the soul. I'd like to now share with you what led up to the 2nd, which was much shorter than the first.

The second dark night of the soul hinged around my mother's passing. She had been one of Jehovah's Witnesses for 50 years at the time of her transition. The doctors say it was lung cancer, yet the decision to leave this life had been made at least 2 years prior, when I reflect on the events surrounding the last few years of my mothers earthly incarnation.

It seemed she had had enough. After faithful service for 48 or so years, she landed in the hospital for another health issue. While there, the doctors diagnosed her with cancer. She was not a smoker, so it was strange. Yet, I felt in my soul it was the result of a decision she'd made to move on from this world. I can't say for sure. It's a gut feeling.

When she transitioned, I was already in a dark place. I had experienced a 2nd divorce, custody issues with our daughter, and a foreclosure of my dream home. My whole life was caving in on me. I was surrounded by failed dreams. My world had morphed into one big disaster. To add to it, mom was getting sicker and sicker by the month. My sister moved back home to take daily care of her, a beautiful gift I appreciate and marvel at to this day.

After the foreclosure of my dream home, I moved into a small apartment with my 2 daughters. My son was now living on his own. Months after being in the apartment, we were evicted. I hadn't been able to pay the rent. I couldn't make money, even though I attempted everything my fragile mind could conjure. I couldn't serve clients as I'd done for years as a spiritual life coach. The income was so low I barely had enough to eke out a living for me and the girls.

I put my things in storage and moved in with a dear friend after the eviction. The dark night of the soul deepened and I questioned life like never before. I couldn't understand why this series of disasters had befallen me (victim thinking) and I had no idea of where I was going next, or what to do about any of it.

Answers eluded me.

I cried every day.

Even still, I kept on filming videos for my YouTube channel and doing the best I could to pull together a couple of coaching programs for clients.

Eventually, I made enough money to get a beautiful apartment in a remote part of town. I didn't have a car, and didn't care. I just needed OUT of my situation ASAP.

I jumped.

Within a few short months of being in the apartment, I had to move again due to not being able to pay the rent. Even though the rent was low, my even lower and inconsistent income couldn't cut it.

I was going down fast. Having to give up the second apartment after an eviction, foreclosure, divorce and custody issues was taking its toll. I was running out of steam.

Mom was getting worse. My siblings and I thought she would pull through. She'd always been an abnormally strong, resilient woman. Blinded by our own unwillingness to let her go, we didn't consider that perhaps she wanted out. We kept reassuring her she'd be well and healed. We all prayed for her recovery non-stop, though that was not the divine plan. She was ready to move on from this world.

When I reflect lovingly on it all now, I realize that mom gave the 4 of her children a precious gift: the time to come to grips with the fact that her days here were done.

We didn't want to accept it, but it was true. She would not make a recovery from cancer. She would leave us. We would be devastated.

Add all that together and you have a glimpse of my state of utter desperation: I was a homeless, broke, sad, grieving daughter, with no answers.

Dark night of the soul number 2.

It lasted 3 years.

I emerged better, stronger, faster, wiser and more joyful than EVER. It wasn't easy. I had to deprogram myself and BE DIFFERENT. Such were the almost unbearable lessons in my soul curriculum. I'm glad to say I did what was required to be free and continue to do it.

Bliss is worth the work.

I share this with you with an intention to impart HOPE and INSPIRATION. When I was in the abyss, I thought there was no way out. That was an illusion. There's ALWAYS a way.

I had to, on both occasions, determinedly and intentionally choose to experience and reach new levels in consciousness to graduate my circumstances. I had to CHOOSE to GO UP.

It's not easy going up. UP is against gravity. There's a default mode to human existence: sliding down. I couldn't keep sliding down. I HAD to push myself UP, no matter how gargantuan the task.

So what is a dark night of the soul?

For me it was being pimp slapped by the universe with disaster that I could not resolve. It was being overwhelmed, pressed further than I could humanly stand. It was the shame of no money and not being further ahead in my life than I thought I should have been for the age I was. It was the pain of being lost and hopeless, and at times, helpless. It was horror and tears and scorn and more than I thought I could endure in a dozen lifetimes. It was experiencing everything I loved slipping through my hands like sand. It was heartbreaking. It was scary. It was sleeping in my car with no place to go. It was the made up story of unbearable loneliness from abandonment. It was hell.

And it was all OVERCOME by the GRACE OF GOD.

No matter how dark, lonely, sad and scary the dark night of the soul is, it can be GRADUATED with HONORS.

Life can be a hard school. My soul chose a curriculum that was agonizing (in divinely ordained spaces and places) for me to learn the deep soul lessons I could learn no other way.

I wouldn't wish any of what I experienced on anyone else. My mission is to inspire to ascend, and graduate dark nights of the soul in elegance and grace, and possibly, to not have dark nights of the soul at all.

Ascending the long, cold, dark night may not be easy, yet it can be done. I promise you.

If you're in a dark night of the soul now, I feel you. I've been there. It was tough.

What I can say to you is this:

GET UP. YOU STILL HAVE MUCH TO DO ON THIS PLANET. THERE ARE ANSWERS. THERE'S A MEANS TO RETURN TO THE BLISS, JOY, BEAUTY AND PERFECTION YOU WERE BORN TO BE.

Let's do this,
Rev. Valerie Love (aka KAISI)

Ascension

In total, I've spent about a decade in dark night experiences, feeling like sh*t. As I write this, I'm 59 years young, so 10 years totals 17% of this incarnation thus far.

In the first dark night I experienced:
- Paralyzing depression
- Painful separation from my family & friends when I chose to exit the cult of Jehovah's Witnesses
- Divorce
- Bankruptcy
- Collapse and loss of my entire world as I knew it
- Consideration of suicide as a viable option

In the second dark night I experienced:
- A 2nd divorce
- Painful custody issues with our daughter
- Mom's transition
- Foreclosure of my dream home
- Eviction
- Homelessness
- Complete financial devastation

While I shared with you that my first dark night of the soul was bought on by soul denial, by the time I experienced the second dark night, I'd made the choice to honor my soul, live my destiny and be and do all I was born for.

After doing that for years, and experiencing the freedom, new community and bliss of being true to me, why had I found myself in yet another abyss?

The answer leads us to yet another reason for the dark night: preparation for ASCENSION. We could say a dark night of the soul is both a pathway to, and a means of ASCENSION.

Not everyone experiences a dark night of the soul, nor does everyone have to. It's quite possible to ascend without it. Conversely, not every dark night is about an immediate ascension. I won't make the statement that I know what every dark night is for, because I do not. The universe is way smarter than me.

The wisdom garnered on the path appeared in the form of divine answers about the unfoldment of my unique soul path on the planet.

You'll have to seek and find those answers for yourself. I'm here to help by sharing my journey. To the extent that it illuminates your journey, use this material to ascend.

I came to learn that a dark night of the soul is an invitation of sorts. For me, the first invitation came because I was living so far from my authentic Self that the soul stood up and made a decision, in concert with my spirit team of angels, ancestors and guides, to wake me up.

I regard it as an invitation into AUTHENTICITY. I didn't have a chance in hell of thriving without being true to Self.

The next dark night was an invitation into POWER. It was a memorable and poignant teacher of truths I HAD to embody: I am not a victim, never have been and never will be, and that if I don't stand up in INNER POWER and act like the Sovereign Creator I AM, I would have a real problem on this planet.

How do I know the 2nd dark night was a lesson in divine power?

Beside the Voice of intuition guiding me from within, I had evidence in my outer world that there were unaddressed and unresolved issues in my consciousness:

- I still felt like a victim. I thought things happened 'to' me from the outside. I thought life meant that we were destined to suffer. This is far from the truth and thus painful.
- I still felt like life's little bitch. At times, I thought I was the whipping girl of the universe. I had not yet realized the power within to intentionally CREATE and MANIFEST the life I desired. Yes, I knew of these ideas and possibilities on a mental level. I had not yet realized these exquisite truths to my core such that I could effortlessly demonstrate them in my world.

I didn't want to keep having that kind of problem, so I got myself together and anchored into POWER within my being.

The power had been there all along. I was afraid of it and terrified to use it.

Fast forward to now.

I don't allow distractions. The work God sent me here to do is too valuable and important for those childhood escapades.

I rescue no one. No one needs rescuing.

I have no need for excess adrenaline. The happy hormones flooding my body feel infinitely more delicious. I get much more done in much less time, and with a light heart.

I surrendered belief in emergencies. I'm thankful they're rare. I don't think we have to have emergencies. It seems the more in the moment I live, the more I pour myself into why I'm here, my SOUL work, the less hectic life becomes.

Living your soul's destiny produces a nectar flavored with beauty and bliss. I call it cosmic orgasm.

How did I change my energetic system? How did I end hopelessness, adrenaline dependency, staggering boredom and a feeling that my life essence was draining out of me?

I had to learn. I had to grow. I had to erase negative patterns that served few good purposes other than provide clarity on what not to do.

One of the many lessons I learned in the dark night of the soul that brought these negative tendencies to an end (mostly because I didn't have the energy to keep doing what I was doing) was that people are just fine without me. Everyone is Source at the true level of Being, which means we all have our own answers. Everyone is going to make it, eventually.

The first dark night revealed to me, viscerally, that my incessant rescuing of everyone and allowing my precious energy to be gobbled up by distractions were just avoidance tactics, providing me with clever ways to procrastinate on the most important thing in my life: **BEING THE REAL ME AND DOING WHAT I CAME TO THE PLANET TO DO..**

I have a question for you...

How long can you run from yourself?

An even more pivotal question:

How long can you run from yourself and expect to be happy, peaceful and fulfilled?

I think you and I both know the answer to that question. The avoidance tactics must stop. The running must end.

The Universe of Life has oh so many wonderful (and not so wonderful) ways of getting us to stop running, stop avoiding, and face SELF.

Trust me, my spirit team was ON IT. They had quite a bit of experiential learning on tap for me. Little did I know that all my crap was about to blow up in my face, which is a really good thing... especially because I had been in it for so long that I had begun to conduct myself as if these dysfunctional patterns were actually me.

I was confused about identity. I was identified with my behaviors.

'Valerie is a rescuer. That's what I do. I save people.'

This was a tragic lie that I had to be rescued from, by the TRUE SELF.

True Self, show me who I am, because clearly I'm mistaken!

My identity was misfigured, misconstrued. I had major identity confusion, which fed into a major identity crisis.

Hence triggering the dark night of the soul.

A necessary lesson, especially for where I was at the time... in my late 20's early 30's, over-busy mom of 2 tiny ones, a husband, a vampiric, demanding religion that was sucking the lifeblood out of me, and in general, an entire inauthentic life.

My religious background did not serve to root me in spirituality. Instead, it mired me in rules. I had no spiritual practices to speak of, such as prayer, meditation, silence, breathing, fasting, nature walking and/or yoga. I had religious practices galore... go to the religion's house, say the words the religion says to say, do the things the religion says to do, hang only with people who are in the religion.

Religiosity attempted to crowd out the inner knowing of the soul. It was unsuccessful. I cannot say it was not without trying as hard as it could to elicit absolute compliance, by seeking to exercise complete ownership and control of me and over me.

What if misplaced religion is the devil? The one we make a pact with to get stuff (friends, 'acceptance', belonging) in exchange for our soul?

It's amazing I got free at all. I call it a miracle.

Yes, as I review it now, my emergence from two dark nights were made possible by a series of miracles.

I learned so much in that darkness. I believe the darkness has more to teach us than we've been led to believe.

It tested the limits of my perceived desperation. In the darkness, I was desperate. Desperate for spiritual oxygen (inspiration), for real belonging (and not to a place or a clan that could kick me out at will), for acknowledgment (not knowing I was called to acknowledge myself). Yes, desperation had taken me hostage more than I'd like to admit.

Desperation for money and trying to take care of me and my 2 kids almost seduced me onto the stripper pole. I have a nice booty, so why not?

I sat outside the club in downtown Baltimore staring at the door from my car, there on an invitation from a man who had almost convinced me that the nightly money would be easy. Do I park my car and go in?

Something in me knew that if I walked through that door, I was going down another path that was not aligned with my highest and best.

For some, the stripper pole is a place of power, and finding oneself. It was for Cardi B. That stripper pole propelled her to unforeseen heights.

For me, it was not to be. Something in me would not let me get out of my car that day. I thank that something in me. It's true, God has limits on how much we can hurt ourselves. It's almost like keeping a toddler away from electricity. There's nothing wrong with electricity, it's a natural part of life. There is something inappropriate about electrical current in the hands of a 2-year-old.

God saw my 2-year-old consciousness about to touch electricity and gently guided me another way.

Thank you God.

Now let's consider a major solution for the dark night of the soul:

INSPIRATION

In the dark night, it's imperative to stay INSPIRED.

First we'll address what inspiration is, then we'll address how to apply it.

Inspiration has many meanings. Here, we'll use this definition:

The inner fire of Spirit or spark of the divine that is a catalyst for elevated mental states, emotions and feelings... from dark to light and from negative to positive, from depressed to energized, from low to high and from can't do to will do.

Inspiration is an inner fire burning in the cauldron of the heart. It's the inner hearth. When the fire is blazing, the whole house is aglow with warmth and comfort. A fire burning out is a signal to add more wood. An empty fireplace on a frigid night is a big problem.

When we're inspired, we feel amazing. We're compelled into action. We're deeply and profoundly moved. We cannot stay idle. We're energized for the work at hand, even if the work is super challenging. Challenges, hardships, dark nights and obstacles do not matter to one who keeps the inner fire blazing bright.

What are the elevated mental states, emotions and feelings we can expect from INSPIRATION?

- Enthusiasm
- Love
- Joy
- Freedom
- Bliss
- Oneness/Connectivity
- Wholeness
- Clarity
- Vibrant Energy
- Playfulness
- Youthfulness
- Humor/Frivolity/Lightness/Laughter
- Holiness, Innocence and Purity
- Magnetism/Super Attractiveness
- Cosmic orgasm

Before we consider how to stay inspired, journal your thoughts, Satori moments, fears, decisions, intentions and all you're feeling right now...

DATE: _____

Journal

Now that we've talked a bit about the dark night of the soul and what it means, what has been your experience?

Write out feelings, emotions, thoughts and any revelations related to these.

Meditate On Elevated Emotions:

- Enthusiasm
- Joy
- Love
- Freedom
- Bliss

- Oneness/Connectivity
- Wholeness
- Clarity
- Vibrant Energy
- Playfulness

- Youthfulness
- Humor/Frivolity/Lightness
- Holiness/Innocence/Purity
- Magnetism/Super Attractiveness
- Cosmic Orgasm

Answer the following questions in 2-3 sentences:

How often do you experience elevated states?

_____
_____
_____
_____

What triggers negative states?

_____
_____
_____
_____

Does your environment promote well-being?

_____
_____
_____

How aware are you of what you're feeling?

_____
_____
_____

What habits can you employ to elevate your emotions?

_____
_____
_____
_____

JOURNAL

JOURNAL

JOURNAL

JOURNAL

JOURNAL

JOURNAL

JOURNAL

JOURNAL

JOURNAL

JOURNAL

JOURNAL

JOURNAL

JOURNAL

JOURNAL

How to Stay Inspired

This workbook and journal will offer you 3 ways to stay inspired:

1. **Stories** - 3 stories of overcoming impossible odds, to win big and miraculously advance are here for inspiration. Dive into each story with the intention to find the core essence of truth that allowed each person to overcome harrowing circumstances.
2. **Principles** - principles are guiding lights that build character. Here you'll find 12 of my favorite life principles for use in ascending the dark night and developing mental toughness.
3. **Journal** - in each section, blank pages are provided so you journal your experience. I'm a big journaler, having done so for over 3 decades. I can tell you definitively that all the ills that would have found a nest in my body have instead been evicted onto the page. Journaling is therapeutic. Chronicle epiphanies, Satori moments and the feelings accompanying them to reach deep into the caverns of your consciousness for the light. It's there. Keep searching for it. The inner fire is ever present and blazing. You need only throw a few logs on.

You could also explore, though not covered here:

1. Breath work - for instantaneous state changes.
2. Yoga - for aligning mind, body, breath, soul and heart.
3. Walking and/or running for an endorphin high.
4. Water - drinking lots of water helps keep my mind and emotions clear.
5. Sun - light is a key to health.

Now let's consider 3 stories of overcoming unimaginable hardship...

Loss

Just six weeks after Augustine graduated from high school, his mother, while standing in the kitchen making his lunch, dropped to the floor and expired from a massive heart attack.

Augustine was devastated.

In an instant, his dreams of going to college for journalism in the fall and becoming a writer were shattered.

He had no idea of what to do, now that all his reasons for living his dreams had just died on the kitchen floor.

Eventually he got himself together enough to go to work at a local paper factory. Doing this kind of work didn't require much of him, not that he had much to give. At least it would garner him a little income until he figured out his next move.

Shortly thereafter, he decided to join the military. As might be expected, because it was war time, Augustine experienced the battlefield.

When he returned from the war, the next 10 years of Augustine's life, as he termed it, were a living hell. He didn't make much money, so he fell deeply into debt trying to support his new wife and their baby. Troubles mounting, he took up the habit of stopping by the bar for a drink each night on his way home. One drink became two, then four, then six.

Before long, his wife, unable to cope with his alcoholic behavior, packed up their daughter and left.

Augustine's life spiraled downward swiftly as he drifted from place to place in his car, a wandering derelict, doing odd jobs to make enough money for the next bottle of cheap wine.

He spent many a night in the gutter.

He hit rock bottom on a cold and wintry day when he stumbled upon a pawn shop where he saw a gun in the window for just $29. He took 3 ten dollar bills out of his pocket (all the money he had) with the intention of buying the gun and ending his life. He told himself he'd no longer have to face the failure staring back at him in the mirror every day. The weight of his life was almost unbearable. He would buy the gun, he thought, and go back to the cheap motel he'd rented for the night and splatter his brains all over the room.

As Providence would have it, and for some inexplicable reason, instead of buying the gun, Augustine turned around and headed in the opposite direction. His wandering landed him at the library, where he entered to escape the frosty winds.

He meandered over to the self-help and success section, where he selected several books. He sat down at a table in the public library and began to read while warming himself. If nothing else, Augustine thought, maybe he would discover why his life was such a mess.

Augustine read and read and read. From that day on, he visited the library frequently. Over the next couple of years, Augustine read hundreds of success books and gradually gave up drinking.

Then Augustine read a book that would forever change his life: *Success Through a Positive Mental Attitude* by W. Clement Stone.

On the book jacket, he read that Mr. Stone owned a company. Augustine applied for work at Mr. Stone's company and was accepted as a salesman. In his new position, Augustine successfully applied and effectively utilized the principles he'd learned from Mr. Stone's book and the hundreds of success books he'd devoured over the years. He was promoted to sales manager within one short year.

Augustine's dream of being a writer never died. With work going so well for him, he decided to take a week off to write. He purchased a typewriter and neatly typed a sales manual. He sent his newly created sales manager to the home office of the company he worked for, praying that someone would recognize his writing talent.

Sure enough, his writing genius was noticed and Augustine was eventually invited by Mr. Stone to be the editor of his magazine. He gave Augustine a blank check along with a charge to make the magazine a nationwide success.

Augustine's excellence exceeded everyone's expectations.

In one issue, Augustine didn't have an article to fill space that needed to be filled. Nothing in the archives was to his liking. So he went home and wrote all night to produce his own article for the magazine. After the article ran, Augustine got a phone call from a major publisher who was so impressed with his writing that he offered to publish his book if Augustine ever decided to write one.

Eighteen months later, Augustine's first book was published: *The Greatest Salesman in the World*.

You may know Augustine by his nickname: Og.

Og Mandino went on to write 21 other books, including *The Greatest Secret in the World*, *The Greatest Miracle in the World* and *The God Memorandum*. His books have sold over 50 million copies and have been translated into over 20 languages.

When I think of Og, I am filled with inspiration. No matter how great the obstacle, when I call to mind Og's homelessness, suicidal despair, alcoholism, loss of his wife and child, and the sudden loss of his mother as a teen, I know there's always hope for a new day.

When I think of Og lying in gutter after gutter, yet having the courage to get up one more time, I am strengthened beyond words.

When I think of Og staring at a gun in a pawn shop window while formulating a plan to end it all, and the miracle of God that turned him away from the pistol and toward the library, I am awed at what God can do in our moments of deepest darkness.

When I think of Og, I remember that there's always a better thought and feeling I can reach for and attain. My success is assured, to the highest degree desired, when I simply shift my thinking. God steps in and does the rest.

Likewise, your success is assured.

I don't know what kind of obstacles you're facing today, they may range anywhere from slight annoyances to serious, down-on-your-knees, monster issues. Whatever it is, there's a path paved just for you that will lead to the highest and most glorious life God ordained for you before the beginning of time.

Keep the faith, even when you feel like you're lying in the gutter, and even if you've seen this gutter before. A massive secret to success is to get up one more time than you fall.

When all else fails, and you have nothing to draw on, remember Og Mandino, a writer with a big vision to change the world, and actually did.

Journal your epiphanies and inspirations...

JOURNAL

JOURNAL

JOURNAL

JOURNAL

JOURNAL

JOURNAL

JOURNAL

JOURNAL

Meaning

Seeing the 'Auschwitz' sign caused panic to wash over them. The newest arriving prisoners knew well the notorious reputation of this camp, a reputation that included torture and execution. No one sent there had returned alive.

However, the newest arrivals at the infamous camp were somewhat relieved when they were met by other prisoners who had already been there. The existing prisoners seemed to be in fairly good condition.

What the new prisoners did not know, nor could have known, was that the existing prisoners who met them were carefully selected for this purpose precisely. The existing prisoners had been able to endure the trials of the camp and still appeared to be in better condition than would be expected.

One of the prisoners recounts one of the worst parts of the ordeal: having his possessions taken and looted. He was not primarily concerned with his possessions. He was mortified that his manuscript had been taken away.

The man was Victor Frankl. His manuscript was on the topic of 'logotherapy,' a therapeutic practice he had developed that helped people find meaning in their lives.

Little did he know at the time that the confiscation of his manuscript would be one of the driving forces that propelled him forward in the concentration camp, keeping him alive and giving his own life meaning.

The cold was biting. Early in the morning Victor and the other prisoners would be forced at the butt of guns to walk miles in freezing temperatures. The yell of 'caps off!' was a particularly painful one. All the prisoners would have to remove their caps to walk with no head covering until the guards allowed them to put their caps on again.

Those whose feet were too blistered and raw to walk leaned on the arms of friends.

While in the camp, it became clear to Victor that he would have to *find meaning* in his horrid experiences if he was to ever walk out of the concentration camp, sane and in the best psychological state one could hope for, considering the horrendous circumstances. It would not be hard to fall into irreversible hopelessness over a meaningless existence when everything around you seems to offer evidence. The captors and surroundings scream 'you don't matter'... 'your life is meaningless'... 'your life can be ended on a whim.'

For 3 years Victor lived in the Nazi concentration camps where he was conscripted into forced labor, digging graves, never knowing if the grave he dug on any particular morning might be the very same grave he would land in that night.

The graves he dug were filled with the bodies of those who were led into the infamous gas chambers, and of those who had met with death in the multiplicity of ways that one could die in a concentration camp: frostbite, hunger, illness, hate at the butt of a gun.

Needless to say, Victor and those who accompanied him lived a harrowing tale of torture, death, and ultimate hatred in Auschwitz.

The good news: he survived.

Maybe Victor didn't imagine that the confiscation of his manuscript would turn out to give him a superpower: a driving and imminent reason to be free so that he could rewrite the book, bringing his logotherapy to the world. As a psychiatrist, Victor was forced to find meaning in his own life, without knowing whether he would survive or not. The beauty of his ultimate tale of triumph and victory is that Victor has since helped millions of people around the globe to find greater meaning in their lives, and the adversities that meet us all. We may not have the adversity Victor faced, yet we all have adversities that test us to the core.

In all he experienced, Victor Frankl never lost sight of the ultimate human gift: ***his freedom***.

Yes, his liberty was hindered because his body was imprisoned, yet his mind was not.

Victor states that the last of all human freedoms is the ability, in any given circumstance, no matter how dire, to **choose one's attitude**.

You are the only one who gets to choose your attitude.

You are the only one who gets to choose what you will think.

The Nazi's had Victor's body, but they never had his mind, nor access to his soul.

He survived to recount his story in the book *Man's Search for Meaning*.

When faced with adversity, choose to remember the gift of your freedom, which is the greatest gift of all: your ability to choose your attitude, to choose what you will think, feel and experience in any given set of circumstances, no matter how dire those circumstances may be.

Remember, you already have the ultimate gift. It was given to you, completely free, by your Creator before you were born.

FREEDOM is your birthright.

Journal your epiphanies and inspirations...

JOURNAL

JOURNAL

JOURNAL

JOURNAL

JOURNAL

JOURNAL

JOURNAL

JOURNAL

Cannibalism

The year was 1846. James Reed, a successful Illinois businessman, got the idea to head west in the great migration of the 1800's, hoping to vastly increase his fortune in the new and rich land of California.

Margaret Reed, James's wife, didn't agree. She was happily satisfied and settled in their beautiful home and couldn't understand why her husband would want to venture out west, away from the comfortable life they had built for themselves.

Eventually, James won and the family headed west. To ensure that they would experience pure luxury and comfort on the treacherous trail, James loaded his wife and four children, his mother-in-law and two of the family's servants into a custom-built two-tiered covered wagon, complete with a built-in iron stove, spring cushioned seats, beds for sleeping, velvet curtains and Margaret Reed's treasured organ. The townspeople gathered in awe as they watched the family depart in a monstrosity of a covered wagon, which required 8 oxen to pull.

Also in the party travelling west were 8 other covered wagons, 32 folks in all. Along the way, several others joined the party, which came to include almost 90 people in over 20 wagons.

The group travelled through treacherous land, mountains and deserts, coming face to face with unexpected troubles along the way. Several of the oxen ran away. Being unable to safely navigate the mountains, Reed and his family had to abandon their palace on wheels.

The group met with an early winter. A blanket of snow began to fall, making it impossible to continue the trek. Supplies were ominously low. Eventually, the group ran out of food.

The elements became deadlier, claiming the lives of more than a few of the travelers.

In desperation, some members of the group resorted to cannibalism.

James Reed made the heartbreaking decision to leave his family behind in search of a rescue party along with supplies.

Death, despair and cannibalism continued to sweep through the camp.

Yet, Margaret Reed and her four children survived without ever resorting to cannibalism. How? Margaret kept herself and her family alive on snow, bark, and pot liquor from boiled leather. This woman, who had been accustomed to the finest things in life, who had lived a posh existence with servants at her beck and call, found within herself a tensile strength that became life-saving. She employed courage, faith, ingenuity and prayer to get her family safely through the crises.

Truly a remarkable woman, with a remarkable story.

When I consider the ill-fated Donner Party, one of the worst faring expeditions in American history, I think of the Reeds, their fortune and what really saved their lives.

I am both James and Margaret. Perhaps you are too.

On one hand, the Margaret Reed in me wants to stay in a comfortable place, clinging to what's familiar, not seeking to venture outside the box; all the while knowing that nothing in the physical realm has saving power when the going gets tough. Sooner or later, the reservoir of tensile strength within must be tapped... the universe will see to it that we get those opportunities.

The James Reed in me wants something more, it's the longing to grow and stretch, to seek opportunity in a new land. It's the part of me that hears the whisper to "come up higher."

This part of me is willing to risk today's comfort for tomorrow's fulfillment.

What about you? Have you made the decision to venture out into unknown territory for the hope of something far better? Do you feel it's landed you in a precarious situation, one that you would not be in had you not ventured beyond the safety of home?

If you haven't made the decision to leave behind your comfortable confines, chew on this: you will leave your self-prescribed and self-imposed comfort zone, one way or the other. You can venture out voluntarily, or you can be presented by Life with learning opportunities, which may be of the most dire type, just as Margaret was.

Soon enough, you'll see what you're made of: tensile strength, courage, holiness and divinity.

Journal your epiphanies and inspirations...

JOURNAL

JOURNAL

JOURNAL

JOURNAL

JOURNAL

JOURNAL

JOURNAL

JOURNAL

12 Mental Toughness Principles

These principles have been a guiding light for me and a solid support to raise myself up to a higher standard.

They have the power to lift you out of the abyss if implemented fastidiously.

What have been the results of my inner transformation by employing these principles and other life changes?

- Profound joy and bliss.
- Financial freedom and abundance.
- Global travel to multiple locales and countries including China, Hong Kong, Dubai, Paris, Cannes, Peru, Mexico, Sedona, Salem, New Orleans and more. (You can guess I love travel!)
- Super loving relationships in which I feel adored and appreciated.
- Vibrant and radiant health and wellbeing. I take no meds, thank you universe!
- Deep satisfaction and abiding fulfillment from living my destiny, the reason I was born into this incarnation.
- The pleasure and privilege of inspiring millions around the globe through my YouTube channel, books, retreats, programs and events.
- More peace than I could have fathomed.

Now let's take on power principles that catalyze mental toughness...

Principle #1: Awareness

The experience and process by which unconscious beliefs and issues surface in the conscious mind so they can be acknowledged, addressed, released and/or healed.

These issues may have lived in the subconscious mind for decades, silently creating your results without your conscious participation. Awareness doesn't always feel good, yet it's the first vital step to creating new and different results.

You cannot transform anything you are unaware of.

Awareness is a first vital step because the universe has a prime directive for us as humans: WAKE UP.

What are we waking up to? To the wondrous awareness of our GOD POWERS.

Ask yourself:

- What am I aware of about the meaning and purpose of this dark night of the soul?
- What am I aware of that requires my loving attention to address and resolve in consciousness?
- What am I willing to be aware of?
- Do I really want to wake up and see my life for what it is?
- Am I ready to make the necessary sweeping life changes that will most certainly be uncomfortable?

JOURNAL

JOURNAL

JOURNAL

JOURNAL

Principle #2: Acknowledgment

Owning all beliefs and issues held in consciousness and their out-pictured results.

Acknowledgment comes after awareness and says: "I created this" (whatever 'this' is), **without even so much as a smidge of judgment.**

You cannot heal or transform any issue without humbly acknowledging its existence as 'cause' in your mind and 'effect' in your life experience.

This does not mean you chose the exact circumstances you have now.

It means we **ALWAYS** get to choose our **ATTITUDE.** We acknowledge that a better attitude will lead to better results, and sour attitudes create after their kind.

We cannot escape the laws of cause and effect, so we may as well take complete responsibility.

Remember, you are never at fault. You are, however, **RESPONSIBLE.**

JOURNAL

JOURNAL

JOURNAL

JOURNAL

Principle #3: Acceptance

Peacefully abiding with, embracing and honoring whatever presents itself as the issue that needs to be addressed and healed at the time, knowing there is inherent perfection and beauty in **EVERY** life experience.

ACCEPTANCE.

Breathe and accept ALL of what you are experiencing right now.

Acceptance does NOT mean agreement.

Acceptance does NOT mean acquiescence.

Acceptance does NOT mean avoidance.

Acceptance is the moment you stop fighting life.

We have what we have for a reason. Acceptance allows us to understand this deeply and be at peace, even if sitting in the middle of a concentration camp.

*When we become **aware** of our issues, **acknowledge** them and **accept** them peacefully, we open the magical door to transformation and a whole new world.*

JOURNAL

JOURNAL

JOURNAL

JOURNAL

Principle #4: Authenticity

You'll remember that a big reason I was in the first dark night of the soul was because I was inauthentic to the soul, the real me.

Authenticity is discovering, uncovering, accepting, embracing, celebrating and sharing the REAL YOU, without reservation, veils, hiding, shrinking or negating self.

It's living your truth from the heart. When you're true to you, being true to everyone else is easy.

Authenticity paves the way for us not to be overly concerned with what people think, and allows us to settle into a peaceful place within that's self-aware, self-assured and self-confident.

The Christ presence bids us to let our light shine. Only an authentic person can masterfully accomplish this charge.

Your authentic life begs expression. You will never be satisfied or fulfilled doing what other people want you to do if it's not in alignment with your soul.

I had to find this out the hard way.

Be true to YOU.

JOURNAL

JOURNAL

JOURNAL

JOURNAL

Principle #5: Choice

Choice is the ability to select our path, actions, behaviors, words and attitudes.

You get to determine how you will be, out of a myriad of possibilities.

Choice narrows the field of infinite possibilities to one path in any given situation, along with all the resulting consequences, wanted or unwanted.

In choice there is power. Where there's power, there's responsibility.

You are solely responsible for your choices. No choice is still a choice, if only by default.

To make the best choices, access divine Mind by intuition or divination. Choice is your sovereign right. Use it well.

JOURNAL

JOURNAL

JOURNAL

JOURNAL

Principle #6: Community

Surround yourself with an unconditionally loving, unconditionally accepting, inspiring group of people who agree to commune around a shared purpose, vision and mission that serves the whole.

A family can be a community, if each member vows to unconditionally love and inspire each other.

There are some gatherings of people that are NOT supportive, and in this spiritual context, would not be called community.

Commune and unity combine to create community. Harmony is fostered in community. Your greatest gifts and accomplishments are discovered and shared in community. You rise to your full and true potential only in community.

Community becomes the sacred soil in which we're planted. If we're honest with ourselves, we'll confess that many of our fall downs occurred when we were left to our own devices, or when we refused to phone a friend, or didn't seek out assistance in a troubling moment.

No one is here to rescue anyone else.

Community is about saying to other beloved and trusted souls "I'm here for you as you do your work and I do mine."

JOURNAL

JOURNAL

JOURNAL

JOURNAL

Principle #7: Courage

Courage is from the French word meaning 'heart' and is about moving forward boldly and powerfully, from the heart and with heart, even with gargantuan fears staring you down or resistance seeking to block you.

It takes extreme courage to create and live your authentic life of destiny fulfilled.

Courageous people are not people who have no fear... they are people who act boldly despite their fears.

Being fearless is not required. Being the kind of person who moves forward ANYWAY is courageous.

JOURNAL

JOURNAL

JOURNAL

JOURNAL

Principle #8: Desire

I define desire as the delicious and expectant knowing and awareness, with happiness and joy, of a greater good that's available to us and has been prescribed for us, placed in the heart by Source.

From the root words: de, meaning 'of the' and sire, meaning 'Father' desires are literally 'of the Father.'

Of course, we are speaking of the impetus of the soul and not passing fancies, lusts, attachments, control or having to have a manifestation show up in a specific way.

Desire is a critical element of reality creation. All achievement began with a burning desire. The greater the burning desire, the more likely it will be accomplished.

It becomes critical for us to access the desires burning within and allow them to manifest through us, if we are to fulfill our potential as light channels on the planet.

When I was in the dark night, desire had vanished. I didn't have a beautiful expectation of greater good.

Fan the flames of your desires and choose to do what's required to fulfill them. This is the deliciousness of life. You're a creator. You can't not create and be happy.

JOURNAL

JOURNAL

JOURNAL

JOURNAL

Principle #9: Enthusiasm

Enthusiasm is derived from en-theos, meaning to be 'in God' or divinely ablaze with passionate zeal for what's good and useful and lawful.

Enthusiasm springs from the Solar Plexus, the inner central sun.

Enthusiasm is deeper than excitement, and is more lasting. Excitement is a hair away from fear. Enthusiasm is fueled by inspiration.

I remember a time when I had nothing to be enthused about. An existence filled with 'have-to's' is not the playing field of enthusiasm.

I came to understand and eventually realize that enthusiasm is not tied to an outer event or circumstance.

Enthusiasm is a decision.

JOURNAL

JOURNAL

JOURNAL

JOURNAL

Principle #10: Expectancy

Expectancy is certainty.

It's an absolute knowing that your good is on the way, as demonstrated by you being fully prepared to receive it. A person who holds a winning lottery ticket is certain of the funds they'll receive, even though the check has not yet arrived. That's expectancy.

Expectancy is a critical element of reality creation and is based on rock solid faith. A faithful person EXPECTS good; therefore, it shows up. Your faith and expectancy call the invisible into the visible. Your expectancy is the demand on the universe to provide its treasures for you in manifested form.

A trap of being in the dark night is not to expect magnificent good.

Do NOT fall into this trap. Your immense good is assured. Be certain. Be confident.

Mental toughness is built on CERTAINTY.

JOURNAL

JOURNAL

JOURNAL

JOURNAL

Principle #11: Gratitude

Be deeply thankful beyond any particular thing or experience.

Gratitude is an overall energy of appreciation for everything as it all exists now, without wanting things to be any different from how they are.

The more grateful we are, the more magnificent life blossoms open for us. We look up to find ourselves in paradise.

Gratitude is an attitude, a way of being, an orientation; not an occurrence based on receiving goodies.

Society has taught us to be grateful only when the desired shows up. We get to be grateful even when the undesirable shows up. At least we're alive to witness it. For this we can be grateful.

True gratitude is happy and thankful all the time as a way of living beyond any particular thing or person.

Gratitude is. Gratitude makes for a rich life and inspires the knowing that there's gold in every adversity.

All things happen for a very good reason. Let's be grateful.

JOURNAL

JOURNAL

JOURNAL

JOURNAL

Principle #12: Love

God is love. Compassion is the action of love. Kindness is the flavor of love.

Love is not a sappy emotion.

Love is the creative essence of this entire universe, the underpinning of all life, the energy holding, healing and sustaining all. Love is impersonal.

Love is the answer to every question, the solution to every problem, the ultimate and only healer. Love is both a principle and a law.

It would be impossible to ascend a dark night without heaping mounds of love upon yourself.

A fave passage of mine from the Holy Bible reads:

"Love suffereth long, *and* is kind; love envieth not; love vaunteth not itself, is not puffed up, **5** doth not behave itself unseemly, seeketh not its own, is not provoked, taketh not account of evil; **6** rejoiceth not in unrighteousness, but rejoiceth with the truth; **7** [b]beareth all things, believeth all things, hopeth all things, endureth all things. **8** Love never faileth..."

1 Corinthians 13:4-8 (ASV)

JOURNAL

JOURNAL

JOURNAL

JOURNAL

A Closing Word

After transformation and transmutation of consciousness, we ascend. This is alchemy of the soul.

Never give up, no matter how dark the night. Think of Og planning to end it all with a $30 gun, or Victor in a corner of the horrid concentration camp trying to find meaning, or me reaching for a bottle of pills to go to sleep and not wake up again... what's common to all these?

We lived. We overcame our own particular hell. We made it through and ascended the mountain to tell the story.

That means you can too.

I love you and thank you for being here,

KAISI (aka Rev. Valerie Love)

About the Author

KAISI (aka Rev. Valerie Love) is an ordained minister of spiritual consciousness, initiated Christian Witch and the author of 25 books on practical spirituality, the occult, Christian Witchcraft and the Magickal Arts & Sciences.

She leads retreats globally and shares with audiences the Spirit path to creating a life of FREEDOM: spiritually, mentally, emotionally, physically and financially.

Visit KAISI online to explore endless possibilities:
www.ValerieLove.com

Videos to set your soul ablaze are available to you at:
www.ValerieLoveTV.com

May I Ask?

If you enjoyed this workbook, would you consider leaving a review on Amazon or Goodreads?

Please share with us a sentence or two about how you used the material here and your results.

THANK YOU!

YOU ARE LOVED!

Made in the USA
Monee, IL
31 January 2022

90340540R00083